W9-DCL-843

Careers in the National Guards' Search

355.3 GRE

32412

Greene, Meg

CAREERS IN THE

NATIONAL GUARDS'

SEARCH AND RESCUE UNITS

Meg Greene

the rosen publishing group's

rosen
central

Published in 2003 by The Rosen Publishing Group, Inc.
29 East 21st Street, New York, NY 10010

Copyright © 2003 by The Rosen Publishing Group, Inc.

First Edition

Library of Congress Cataloging-in-Publication Data

Greene, Meg.
Careers in the National Guards' search and rescue units / Meg
Greene.—1st ed.
        p. cm. — (Careers in search and rescue operations)
Summary: Discusses the history of the National Guard's Search and Rescue
units, requirements of becoming a member of one of these units, and the role
Guardsmen played after the events of September 11, 2001.
Includes bibliographical references and index.
ISBN 0-8239-3836-0 (library binding)
1. United States. Air Force—Search and rescue operations—Juvenile
literature. 2. United States. Army—Search and rescue operations—Juvenile
literature. 3. United States—National Guard—Vocational guidance—Juvenile
literature. 4. United States National Guard Bureau—Vocational guidance—
Juvenile literature. [1. United States—National Guard—Vocational guidance.
2. Rescue work—Vocational guidance. 3. Vocational guidance.]
I. Title. II. Series.
UG633 .G764 2003
355.3'7'0973—dc21

                                                              2002013246

Manufactured in the United States of America

CONTENTS

INTRODUCTION   September 11, 2001   4

CHAPTER 1   Citizen-Soldiers: The
                Army National Guard   14

CHAPTER 2   Flying High: The Air
                National Guard   24

CHAPTER 3   Joining the Guard   31

CHAPTER 4   "These Things We Do
                So Others May Live"   43

                Glossary   54

                For More Information   57

                For Further Reading   58

                Bibliography   59

                Index   62

INTRODUCTION

September 11, 2001

It had barely been twenty-four hours since the horrific terror-ist attacks in New York City and Washington, D.C. In a brief statement issued to the press on Wednesday, September 12, 2001, Lieutenant General Russell C. Davis, chief of the National Guard Bureau, headquartered in Arlington, Virginia, informed the waiting reporters: "As a result of yesterday's acts of terrorism, tens of thousands of National Guard members across our nation are actively serving or standing ready to serve at the discretion of each state governor."

Lieutenant General Davis was not exaggerating. Only hours after the devastating attacks on the World Trade Center in New York City and the Pentagon just outside Washington, D.C., more than 3,900 National Guard security forces were ready to serve and protect. Of that number, approximately 1,500 troops were already on their way to New York City. Some guardsmen who happened to be in the area or in

A member of the National Guard stands watch near the site of the collapsed World Trade Center towers in New York City. These guardsmen are often called upon to assist in search and rescue operations at disaster sites.

neighboring boroughs, such as the Bronx, were on the scene within minutes of the attacks.

The attacks themselves were unimaginable. At 8:48 AM, a hijacked passenger jet, American Airlines Flight 11 out of Boston, Massachusetts, crashed into the north tower of the World Trade Center, tearing a gaping hole in the building and setting it afire. Less than twenty minutes later, at 9:03 AM, a second hijacked airliner, United Airlines Flight 175 from Boston, crashed into the south tower of the World Trade Center and exploded. A little over an hour later at 10:05 AM, the south tower collapsed, plummeting into the streets below. At 10:28, the north tower fell. A massive cloud of dust and debris formed and slowly drifted away from the wreckage, while fires broke out around the scene.

Thousands of men and women were unaccounted for in the rubble of the WTC. Local firefighters, police officers, and other emergency personnel were already on the scene, doing all they could to find survivors and retrieve the bodies of those who had lost their lives. But they needed help. To aid the search and rescue efforts, the National Guard responded with more than 200 specially trained engineers, and an additional 400 members of the National Guard were on standby waiting to be called in if additional help was necessary.

The National Guard also supplied numerous pieces of heavy equipment and special trucks to clear and haul away debris, as well as medical, military, and transportation vehicles. The terrorist attacks also marked the first appearance of a new National Guard unit: the Civil Support Team (CST), which helped to identify any hazardous materials related to the disaster to which rescue workers and residents of New York City might be exposed. The team was made up of twenty-two full-time Army and Air National Guard members in fourteen different military occupational specialties, including communications and medicine. The team members spent their first eighteen hours on the ground sampling air to make sure no biological or chemical contaminants were present. They also provided communications support to Federal Bureau of Investigation agents in the area, including satellite communications, e-mail, telephone, and radio support.

For the next several weeks, members of the National Guard worked at a variety of rescue and recovery tasks. Some, such as New York Army National Guard sergeant Norberto Berrios, who is an engine mechanic, spent the first three days after the tragedy searching nearby rooftops for parts of the two airliners that crashed into the World Trade Center. When asked to describe his experience for an article entitled "Determined Guard" for the National Guard Bureau Web site, Berrios told the reporter, "Nothing can prepare you for what we've seen during the last week."

In response to the terrorist attacks of September 11, the Army National Guard and Air National Guard formed part of the biggest deployment of National Guard troops in the history of the United States. More than 9,000 guard members were already in service to the governors of their states at the time the attacks took place. Three days after the attacks, President George W. Bush asked that an additional 50,000 guard and reserve troops be mobilized to help in Operation Noble Eagle, the code name given by United States military officials for the guard's role in the war against terrorism.

Operating from a command post at Liberty Island State Park, members of the New Jersey Army National Guard aided New York officials and guardsmen by carefully examining the

In the days following the terrorist attacks in New York on September 11, 2001, National Guard troops assisted the New York City Police Department's effort to maintain order by patrolling the streets in armored vehicles.

truckloads of mangled steel that were once cars, trucks, or pieces of buildings. Many of the New Jersey guardsmen called to active duty in the aftermath of September 11 recalled how they used to see the World Trade Center towers every day. When asked why he was there, Major Dan Mahon replied to the reporter for the National Guard Bureau Web site: "These are Americans. These are our neighbors." For Mahon and the other guardsmen, coming to New York City was more than an act of duty or a show of patriotism. It was also an expression of sympathy for fellow citizens in a time of sorrow and crisis.

In the wake of September 11, the National Guard needed to assume many roles and responsibilities. The members of the 204th Combat Engineering Battalion, who usually build houses and schools throughout the world, instead helped to clean up debris or stood guard in the area around Ground Zero. Members of other guard units escorted city residents to and from the buildings in which they lived and worked. Working in twelve-hour shifts, guardsmen also helped rescue workers remove bucket after bucket of rubble from the World Trade Center site.

Along with other rescue and recovery workers, the guardsmen experienced intense sadness from seeing so much destruction and death. Specialist Patrick Kelley, who was attached to the 204th, told a writer for the National Guard Bureau Web site, "I am still trying to soak everything up. There are times when I become very sad, when the reality of what happened sets in."

Some guardsmen took part in the even grimmer task of removing bodies from the rubble. Specialist Jim Johnson, a member of the New York Army National Guard, D Company, stopped by his unit's armory on the day the attacks occurred. When he first heard the news, Johnson, a medic, volunteered to work in a temporary morgue that New York municipal authorities had created near Ground Zero. In an interview for an article that appeared on the National Guard Bureau Web site, entitled "NY Guard Soldiers at Ground Zero," Johnson told a reporter, "It's rough to move the bodies, because they are fellow New Yorkers. It hits close to home."

Sergeant Melvin Garcia of Headquarters Company, 101st Company of the New York Army National Guard, discovered part of a leg and a torso while working at the site. As he recalled for the same article in which Johnson was quoted, "All I thought about was getting out of there." Although Garcia had worked in an army medical unit and was no stranger to the violence and destructiveness of war, he was overcome by what he saw at Ground Zero. He told the reporter, "I'm a medic, but it sickens me."

Besides the nerve-racking work of searching for survivors and removing the remains of the dead, the guardsmen, like other rescue workers, had to constantly be concerned about placing themselves at personal risk. The collapse of the towers had weakened a number of nearby buildings. The threat of other buildings collapsing was a very real danger. Often during the course of the rescue and recovery mission, workers were forced to "range walk," which found them walking through designated areas of Ground Zero (that were thought to be safe) to search for the missing. In some cases, they had to quickly leave Ground Zero to escape being injured or killed by buildings collapsing or wreckage shifting.

At the same time that the two hijacked planes crashed into the World Trade Center, another hijacked plane, American Airlines Flight 77, slammed into the west side of the Pentagon, the command center of the United States military. The effect was chilling. Toxic black smoke poured from the crash site as numerous fires broke out. To make a bad situation worse, the smoke and heat made navigating the dark halls of the building difficult. With the conditions as they were, many Pentagon workers were virtually trapped inside the building. For many people, the Pentagon crash was beyond imaginable, because it was believed that the building was practically indestructible.

Despite the obvious danger, two Army National Guard medics—Master Sergeant James Smith and Major Gary McKay— who were attending a meeting at the Pentagon, crawled and groped their way to the crash site in the hope of helping survivors to safety. Crawling on their stomachs and holding wet T-shirts to their mouths so they could breath, Smith and McKay slowly made their way through the smoky halls. There they encountered human chains of eight to ten people holding onto each other as they tried to escape. Meanwhile, others were yelling and dragging people from their demolished offices.

Describing his experience to a local television reporter, Master Sergeant Smith said of those whom he had helped to rescue: "They were glad somebody could find them. A lot of them couldn't see because of the smoke in their eyes. They couldn't breathe." Smith added, "It's lucky we [he and McKay] were at the right place at the right time to help other people."

After clearing the halls, Smith and McKay turned their attention to the injured who were in the center courtyard. Smith, a nurse and emergency medical technician, remembers inserting an IV (a device used to administer an intravenous injection of

Members of the National Guard monitor a checkpoint outside the New York Stock Exchange on September 16, 2001. They were posted there to make sure that no unauthorized people entered the building.

medicine) into a badly burned man. McKay, a physician's assistant, treated a woman suffering from severe smoke inhalation.

The efforts of the National Guard did a great deal to restore security and confidence in the aftermath of the terrorist attacks. The guardsmen also proved to be tremendously helpful in the massive rescue and recovery and cleanup efforts that took place in the days and weeks after September 11.

But the presence of the National Guard at the World Trade Center and the Pentagon also served as an important reminder of why the United States depends on these citizen-soldiers. They are often the first line of defense, and because they work with both state and federal agencies, they are often called upon to perform whatever task is at hand. The men and women of the National Guard are volunteers, many of whom have special skills and training, and who willingly give their time and talents to help wherever help is needed. One New York guardsman, busy hauling debris from Ground Zero, summed up the attitude of many when he told a National Guard reporter: "It's not only my duty—it's for the redemption of my city, state, and country."

CHAPTER 1

Citizen-Soldiers: The Army National Guard

The National Guard is older than the United States itself. The guard began on December 13, 1636, when the General Court of Boston, Massachusetts, ordered that all men of military age living in the region were to be grouped into three militia regiments. These regiments were then charged to protect and defend settlements in the colony against attack. Since the seventeenth century, the National Guard has taken part in every conflict in which first the British colonies and then the United States have been engaged.

Soon after the action of the General Court of Boston, other colonies, notably Virginia, Maryland, and Connecticut, also organized militias of their own. In order to be ready if called, the members of the militia met several times a month to drill. Each member was expected to provide his own arms, ammunition, and equipment. In time, British colonial authorities also began calling on the militia to reinforce the troops of the regular British army. While aiding British regulars in their fight

A Gift from England

The idea of a militia originated as early as AD 1016, when the Saxons in England first called upon all able-bodied men to protect king and country from invaders. The concept of the citizen-soldier traveled across the Atlantic with the English settlers who came to the New World. As a result, the citizen-soldier has been part of the American experience from its beginnings.

against the French during the French and Indian War, the American militiamen received valuable combat experience that would later aid them against the British during the War for Independence.

Nevertheless, colonial militias had problems. Many members were rather wild and undisciplined, using the occasion of militia drills to drink and fight. The militia also often faced a critical shortage of weapons. Even more upsetting to colonial leaders, militiamen commonly fled during battle or failed to show up when and where they were most needed. For these reasons, wrote John K. Mahon in *History of the Militia and National Guard*, influential figures such as Benjamin Franklin thought that militias were "of little or no use."

Serving Their Country

By the time the War of Independence began in 1775, more than 164,000 militiamen from all thirteen colonies answered the call to serve in the Continental army. Without the help of the colonial militias, it is doubtful that the Americans would have defeated the British. The colonial militias not only fought in many of the major battles of the war but also raided British supply depots and harassed British forces. Today, thirty-one Army National Guard units carry battle streamers along with their flags during parades and other ceremonial occasions. Each streamer is embroidered with the names of the battles in which their units participated during the War of Independence.

One of the first laws the federal government passed was the Militia Act of 1792. The law said that each state was required to enroll men between the ages of eighteen and forty-two into companies, regiments, and brigades of a state militia. In addition, each state was to appoint an adjutant general and brigadier inspectors. By 1804, the state militias grew to 25,000 volunteers. More than 489,000 militiamen responded to the call during the War of 1812, coming to the aid of the United States Army, which at the time was barely 10,000 men strong.

The National Guard: Beginnings

On August 25, 1824, a New York militia unit adopted the name National Guard. The new name came about as the result of the

An Old and Proud Institution

The oldest military units in the United States are all part of the National Guard. They are the 181st and 182nd Massachusetts Infantry, the 101st Massachusetts Artillery, and the 101st Massachusetts Engineer Battalion. These units are also among the oldest military units in the world.

Marquis de Lafayette's visit to New York. Lafeyette was the French hero of the American Revolution. In a show of respect for Lafayette and his command of the French militia—which was called the Garde Nationale—the New York militia unit adopted the name the Battalion of National Guards. From then on, all state militias became known as the National Guard.

National Guard units continued to support the regular army throughout the nineteenth century. Militia units fought on both the Union (North) and Confederate (South) sides during the Civil War, with more than one million militiamen fighting for the North alone. Estimates also suggest that approximately 90 percent of Union and Confederate forces were made up of members of various state militias. After the end of the war, the National Guard was reorganized with 90,000 men serving as volunteers.

The National Guard went into action again at the outbreak of the Spanish American War in 1898. Approximately 165,000 men volunteered for duty, but only a few guard units saw combat. Several other guardsmen later went to the Philippines to help put down the Philippine insurrection.

The Guard in the Twentieth Century

A more modern National Guard began to emerge in 1903 when Congress passed the Dick Act, also known as the Efficiency of Militia Bill. The bill, named after Major General Charles W. Dick, commander of the Ohio Division of the National Guard and a member of the U.S. House of Representatives, established new standards and guidelines for the National Guard. Under this law, the federal government was required to play a more active role in organizing, training, and equipping the National Guard. The government believed that the best way to accomplish this was to use the same standards as those applied to the United States Army. The law also increased federal funding available to the guard, but to be eligible for federal monies, units needed to maintain a minimum number of volunteers and agree to inspections by regular army personnel. Members of the guard were to attend twenty-four drills a year and undergo five days of annual training.

The Rough Riders

Of the National Guard units sent to Cuba during the Spanish American War in 1898, none was more famous or colorful than the Rough Riders. Though the unit was under the command of General Leonard Wood, the real leader of the Rough Riders was Lieutenant Colonel Theodore Roosevelt. Formally known as the 1st U.S. Volunteer Cavalry, the Rough Riders were at the center of the fighting at the Battle of San Juan Hill, fought on July 1, 1898. The fame of the unit and its commander rested on a bold, if somewhat reckless, charge up Kettle Hill. Roosevelt emerged unhurt, but nearly 100 of his men were killed or wounded. Although he later went on to become the twenty-sixth president of the United States, Roosevelt later wrote in his memoirs that the Battle of San Juan Hill was "the greatest day" of his life.

Just thirteen years later, the government passed the National Defense Act of 1916, considered one of the most important pieces of legislation in the history of the National Guard. Under the law, the militia was transformed from individual units of the states into one large reserve unit of the U.S. Army. The law also made the term "National Guard" mandatory for all state militias. In addition, all units had to be federally recognized, and the qualifications for officers were now set by the War Department. This included opening up the army's schools for the officers of the National Guard to ensure that they would be properly trained.

The act also increased the number of annual training days to fifteen and the number of yearly drills to forty-eight. For the first time, the government authorized pay for all guardsmen who completed their responsibilities. Finally, with the passage of the National Defense Act of 1920, the National Guard was

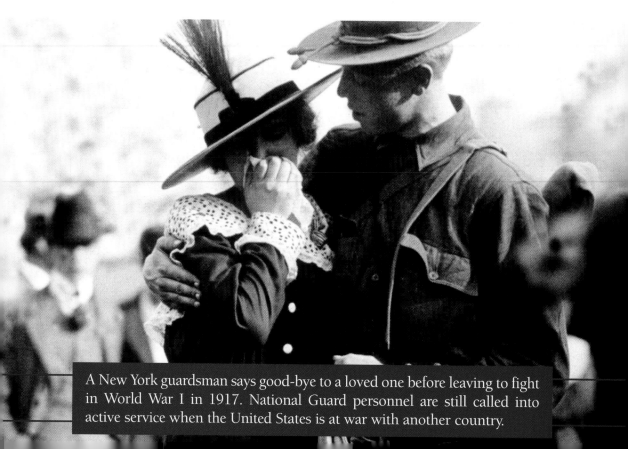

A New York guardsman says good-bye to a loved one before leaving to fight in World War I in 1917. National Guard personnel are still called into active service when the United States is at war with another country.

recognized as a part of the army of the United States when called into federal service. In the meantime, the National Guard remained under the command of state authorities.

During the twentieth century, the National Guard further distinguished itself through its service in every major conflict, including World War I (1914–1918), World War II (1939–1945), the Korean War (1950–1953), the Vietnam War (1964–1969), and Operation Desert Storm (1990–1991). Guardsmen have also served with peacekeeping forces in Bosnia and have been instrumental in the war on terrorism since the events of September 11, 2001. Several hundred citizen-soldiers supported the cleanup and search and rescue operation in New York City alone. Many of the New York National Guard troops supporting the massive recovery operation at Ground Zero in lower Manhattan were from the neighboring Bronx. Guardsmen have also contributed significantly to the national defense by providing airport security.

Since the 1970s, the National Guard has been utilized more for other kinds of duties than for combat. During natural disasters such as floods, tornadoes, and blizzards, state officials have called on their National Guards to keep public order and to assist with recovery and rescue missions. Guardsmen are also no strangers to man-made disasters, responding to everything from energy blackouts to civil unrest.

As of 2000, approximately 350,000 men and women served in the National Guard, consisting of ten active army divisions and fifteen Army National Guard brigades. The brigades trained and modernized in an effort to be compatible with regular army divisions in terms of guard training, equipment, and vehicles. All were fully operational by 2001. The various brigades include seven heavy armored and mechanized brigades, seven light infantry brigades, and an armored cavalry unit.

Members of Missouri National Guard 35th Tank Company undergo combat training in September 1941.

By 2002, the Army National Guard was better trained and equipped to handle state or national emergencies than at any time in its long history. As a result of the $15.2 billion budget received in 2001—the largest ever given to the guard—the National Guard enacted a variety of improvements in training, equipment such as new Blackhawk helicopters and air ambulances, weaponry including state of the art missiles and other artillery, and communications systems. These improvements ensured that the National Guard was prepared for any eventuality. While the United States government depends on the guard to help protect the nation, citizens throughout the nation look to the guard in times of distress.

An Important Component

Today's Army National Guard makes up 44 percent of the total U.S. Army combat divisions and 53 percent of its maintenance units, while the Air National Guard makes up 43 percent of the U.S. Air Force combat and support units. The integration of National Guard units into the army and air force has resulted in many National Guard units being regularly engaged in real world ongoing military missions, such as the peacekeeping operations in the Balkans and air patrols over Iraq.

Chapter 2
Flying High:
The Air National Guard

The Air National Guard is a unique military force. Like the Army National Guard, when not needed by the federal government, the units of the Air National Guard are commanded by the governor of each state and are recognized separately from the air force. Each unit, however, is also attached to an air force command that provides additional leadership and that evaluates each unit's readiness. The Air National Guard units can be called into service by the president or ordered to active duty by Congress.

The Air National Guard is the fifth largest air force in the world after the U.S. Air Force, the U.S. Naval-Marine Corps air forces, the Russian air force, and the air force of the Chinese People's Liberation Army. Like its army counterpart, the Air National Guard is also equipped with the best and most modern aircraft, weaponry, and technology available.

Each of the fifty-four Air National Guard organizations provides emergency relief during natural disasters such as floods, earthquakes, and forest fires. They also engage in search and rescue operations, support civil defense authorities, maintain vital public services such as communications and transportation, and intercept illegal drug shipments. In 2002, the Air National Guard had more than 106,000 officers and enlisted personnel. They served in 88 flying units and 280 independent support units, such as engineering and communications, weather reporting, and security. In addition, the Air National Guard has three rescue and recovery squadrons that fly HH-60 helicopters and HC-130 aircraft.

Pilots of the Vermont Air National Guard fly their F-16 Fighting Falcons in formation over Vermont on August 10, 1998. Members of the squad patrolled the northeastern airspace for several months after the September 11, 2001, terrorist attacks.

The special units provide important lifesaving services to civilian and military agencies.

Origins

Although not as old as the Army National Guard, the Air National Guard was created in the same spirit as the first militia units. The guard's first efforts in aviation took place in 1911 when the First Company Signal Corps of New York became the first National Guard unit to put a plane in the air. Shortly after this experiment, units in Missouri and California created their own flying units. Finally, in 1915, another New York National Guard unit—the 1st Aero Company—received federal recognition as an aviation unit. The 1st Aero Company saw action the following year when called to active duty with the rest of the Army National Guard. In 1921, Minnesota became the first state to establish an Air National Guard squadron. The following year, the 104th Squadron of the Maryland National Guard became the first unit to have its own aircraft.

In the months before the American entry into World War II, President Franklin D. Roosevelt called a number of Air National Guard units to active duty. Many of these units saw combat duty in the Pacific, European, and Mediterranean theaters of operation. Although some units flew bombing missions, the majority of Air National Guard planes carried out reconnaissance, gathering information on enemy troop deployments and weather conditions. Yet it was common for the army air force, the forerunner of

Up in the Air

The first attempt at aviation for military purposes came during the American Civil War. On May 31, 1862, two Rhode Island National Guardsmen launched a hot air balloon. They used the balloon to observe Confederate troop movements just before the First Battle of Bull Run. This effort marked the first time military surveillance by air was conducted in the United States.

the air force, to search the various Air National Guard units when they needed additional pilots and aircrews to man their planes.

Between 1950 and 1953, the Air National Guard saw extensive duty in the Korean War when they were called in to help the air force, which was extremely short of planes. During the 1950s and 1960s, National Guard pilots flew reconnaissance missions in Europe, and other units were ready to go into action should the Cold War with the Soviet Union suddenly turn hot and a nuclear war was declared. In 1968, at the height of the Vietnam War, National Guard pilots were mobilized and saw action both on combat and search and rescue missions. On October 25, 1983, Air National Guard units took part in Operation Urgent Fury, the invasion of the small island nation of Grenada. In Operation Just

Cause, which lasted from December 20, 1989, to January 11, 1990, the Air National Guard helped to capture Manuel Noriega, the military dictator of Panama. In 1990–1991, the Air National Guard served in Operation Desert Storm, the code name for the war against Iraq, and is currently active in the war on terrorism.

Rescue and Recovery

In addition to providing combat-ready air units, the Air National Guard has taken on numerous types of missions, including coastal

In 1997, Colorado governor Roy Romer (shown here at the Buckley Air National Guard Base near Denver, Colorado) ordered his state's Air National Guard to inspect the conditions of a state road following a heavy snowstorm.

SARs

SAR (search and rescue) missions began during World War II. In August 1943, twenty-one people abandoned a disabled C-46 cargo plane over an uncharted jungle near the China-Burma border. The crash site was so remote that the only means of getting help to the survivors was by parachutists being dropped to the site. Lieutenant Colonel Don Fleckinger and two medical corpsmen volunteered for the assignment, marking the first time a pararescue was carried out. This event illustrated the need for a highly trained rescue force, and it was with this in mind that the parajumpers, or PJs, were born.

Rescues since then have occurred in virtually every corner of the world. Some of the most heroic stories about the PJs came during the Vietnam War. On a daily basis during the war, PJs risked their lives flying over hostile territory to find friendly forces needing aid. They rode a rescue hoist cable into the Vietnamese jungle to aid wounded infantrymen and injured pilots whose aircraft had been shot down. The aircraft used for these missions, the HH-3 helicopters, also known as the Jolly Green Giants because of their color, are still in use today for all kinds of rescue missions.

search and rescue. To help with these operations, the Air National Guard has created two aerospace rescue and recovery groups, one based in Long Island, New York, the other in northern California. These units take on some of the most daring and complicated rescue missions ever faced by any search and rescue team. In fact, they specialize in difficult rescue missions.

The three Aerospace Rescue and Recovery Group (ARRG) units are always on call and can be ready at a moment's notice. The guardsmen who answer these rescue calls are an elite group, and they are among the most highly trained specialists in the Air National Guard. Known as pararescue jumpers, they undergo rigorous training in order to perform their duties. The PJs (another name for the pararescue jumpers) are few in number; there are approximately 400 scattered throughout the world. They include parachutists, open-water divers, and emergency paramedical technicians.

The PJs also receive training in survival skills, which allows them to work under the most intimidating and difficult conditions, such as in deserts, mountains, jungles, and even the ocean. Many people in the military consider the PJs to be on the same level as Army Green Berets and Navy SEALs because they have all undergone similar training and have similar expertise. Each ARRG unit contains approximately twenty PJs who work with the other pilots, technicians, and support specialists in coordinating and conducting rescue missions. But before becoming a PJ or any kind of specialist, they all start out as new recruits in basic training.

CHAPTER 3

Joining the Guard

Both the Air National Guard and the Army National Guard include men and women from all walks of life. Because of the diverse background of its recruits, the Army National Guard has established an enlistment system that is broad and flexible and that allows recruits to pick when they wish to enlist and what kinds of training they will receive. Talking with a National Guard recruiter is the best way to learn about available opportunities.

Qualifications and Enlistment

Both the Army National Guard and the Air National Guard have two different sets of qualifications for those interested in enlisting: Applicants who have no previous military service must be between the ages of seventeen and thirty-four; applicants who have previously served in the military must be in a position to complete at least twenty years of service in the guard.

All applicants, regardless of racial, ethnic, or religious background, must have completed high school or received an equivalency certificate such as a GED. The guard allows high school seniors to enlist nine months prior to their graduation and to begin their term of service after graduating. All guard applicants must be native-born or naturalized citizens

Though it is possible to enlist in the National Guard in high school, some students, such as sixth grader Elizabeth Christian, are already learning about what kind of training cadets undergo.

of the United States, legal immigrants, or those who possess a green card, or permanent resident card, which is issued by the Department of Immigration and Naturalization.

Because of the physical and mental demands that are involved in being a member of the guard, every applicant must undergo a complete medical examination. The guard also wants men and women of "good moral character" and will not accept applicants who have a history of juvenile delinquency, criminal conduct, drug use, or any other behavior that might potentially cause disciplinary problems or compromise service in the guard. In addition, all potential recruits are required to take the Armed Services Aptitude Battery (ASVAB), a special examination designed to determine the sort of jobs for which an individual might best be suited.

Programs, Incentives, and Benefits

A number of different programs exist for those who are finally accepted into either the Air or Army National Guard. The Army National Guard offers enlistments of three, four, six, or eight years for both men and women. There are also two-, four-, or five-year options for those who opt for the Individual Ready Reserve (IRR) or the Inactive National Guard (ING). Those interested in joining the Air National Guard can choose from six years of active guard duty or four years in the IRR.

Patriotism Calling

Since the events of September 11, 2001, the Army National Guard has seen a sharp increase in the number of people wishing to join. Calls come from both those with previous military experience and those with no military background. On September 4, for example, a week before the attacks, recruiters received 126 calls for information. On September 14, just three days after the attacks, the number of calls had risen to 537.

For those interested in joining the Air or Army National Guard, the first step is to talk with a National Guard recruiter, who can provide information and explain the steps involved in the enlistment process. A recruiter can also discuss benefits such as retirement plans or special pay for hazardous duty, and special programs such as the GI Bill, which helps to pay for college education, or provides a cash bonus for enlisting. Because they are first and foremost under the jurisdiction of the states, each National Guard unit may have different opportunities.

What happens next is that the recruiter makes sure that applicants are eligible to join the National Guard and that they meet all requirements. Individuals then complete a formal application to the guard so that it can do a background check on applicants. Usually, this application asks for information on where applicants have lived, their employment history, and their criminal and military records if relevant. Applicants also undergo their physical exams and their ASVAB examinations at this time to make sure there are no serious health problems and to see which employment and educational areas they might be best suited for. Based on the test results, a career counselor discusses possible career options with each new recruit, who selects an occupation and schedules an enlistment date. The final step involved in joining the National Guard is signing an oath swearing allegiance to the United States and the recruit's current home state. Each new recruit then plans to attend basic training.

Basic Training

Once individuals successfully complete the initial enlistment process for either the Army or Air National Guard, they then enter what is called active duty training (ADT), which continues for a minimum of twelve weeks. Men and women have the same training period, though the basic requirements differ.

For men entering the Army National Guard, basic training lasts for eight weeks, followed by at least four weeks of advanced training. For men entering the Air National Guard, basic training lasts for six weeks, followed by another six weeks of advanced training. Depending on the area in which recruits have decided to specialize, such as communications, aircraft maintenance, intelligence, or medical training, they may spend a longer period in advanced training, especially in fields requiring a great deal of technical expertise such as electronics. Women entering the guard undergo a period of basic training that lasts eight weeks, followed by at least four additional weeks of specialized training.

Training Opportunities

In general, the National Guard provides three kinds of training: recruit training, job training, and continuing education. Although basic training differs between the Air and Army National Guard, both branches share some common traits.

Basic training provides an overall orientation to military life. When new recruits arrive at camp, they are divided into groups of between forty to eighty people. They meet their drill instructors, who will teach them the basics of becoming a soldier. New recruits also receive uniforms and equipment, and then they move into housing, known as barracks, where they live in a dormitory setting. Every day is carefully regimented. Recruits rise early every morning. Their days are filled with field instruction, classes, and exercise. They take all meals together in the main dining hall, which is also known as the mess hall. Recruits undergoing basic training have limited free time.

As the recruits move through basic training, they eventually master the important skills they will need to perform their duties. They also work hard to discipline themselves mentally and physically by completing an intense program of daily exercise and conditioning. Not only do these activities improve recruits' overall fitness and stamina, but they are designed to

Members of the Oregon Army National Guard move to secure a room during an urban war game training exercise. National Guard members are sometimes called into duty during civil disturbances and hostage crises.

teach them how to survive and function under the most difficult of circumstances. Many recruits also find that they form close friendships with those who have completed basic training with them. After basic training, recruits then move on to whatever specialized training they require.

Members of a New York National Guard infantry unit participate in a combat-training exercise on hilly, wooded terrain on the Clinton County Fairgrounds in Plattsburgh, New York.

PJ Training

One of the most demanding training regimens in the Air National Guard is reserved for those who wish to become the parachute jumpers who carry out search and rescue missions. Their exhaustive training program, known as the Pipeline, is an eighteen-month course that begins at Lackland Air Force Base in Texas with eight weeks of demanding physical and mental training.

Recruits run, swim, exercise, and study under the watchful eyes of their drill instructors. At the end of this period, the washout rate stands at 90 percent. Out of classes that average seventy-five recruits, for example, only seven or eight make it to the next phase of training. Another four-week period of intensive training follows at the Combat Diver's School, which is conducted by the Army Special Forces at a base in Key West, Florida. Recruits then travel to Washington State for four weeks to learn how to carry out search and rescue missions in the mountains.

Then comes a three-week training course at Fort Benning, Georgia, with the Army Jump School. Here recruits learn how to parachute. Training concludes with a six-week medical course at Kirtland Air Force Base in New Mexico, at which the PJs learn emergency medical skills.

From Clerical to Combat

For many men and women, joining the Air or Army National Guard opens up a world of possibilities. The guard offers more than 2,000 job specialties spread among twelve broad occupational groups. These include human services, media affairs and public relations, health care, engineering, science and technology, administration, vehicle and machine maintenance, electronics, construction, machine operation, transportation, material handling, and combat.

For many people, training in a field enables them to find work in civilian life. For example, medical training received in the guard may lead to a job in a hospital, a clinic, or with the emergency rescue squad. Computer training may lead to excellent opportunities to work in business or education.

Women in the Guard

While women have been active in the National Guard since the 1950s, it was not until Operation Desert Storm that opportunities for women expanded. New duties for women included some that put them in direct combat, such as fighter and helicopter pilots and command positions, which exposed some female leaders to direct enemy fire. During the Gulf War, hundreds of guardswomen were deployed to Saudi Arabia, where they performed various tasks to support the allied effort. Of the thirty-four active-duty guard members who died in the Gulf War, eight were women.

A National Guard soldier holds an M-16 rifle as she stands guard at San Francisco International Airport on October 5, 2001.

A Quick Breakdown

According to 1999 government figures, most of the women who enlist in the National Guard enter two main occupational areas: 41 percent opt for functional support, which includes administrative and clerical duties, while 16 percent receive some sort of medical training. Enlisted men mostly enter the infantry (21 percent) or electrical/mechanical equipment repair (19 percent). Growing numbers of women, however, are entering nontraditional fields such as infantry (4.3 percent), electronic repair (2.3 percent), and communications and intelligence (3.9 percent).

Today, women comprise about 10 percent of the guard, or approximately 35,000 soldiers. They serve all over the world and carry out a variety of duties. Since the Gulf War, women have also taken on key leadership positions in the guard. In 1991, Wisconsin's Sharon Vanderzyl was promoted to brigadier general, becoming the first flag officer in the Army National Guard. In 1997, Lieutenant Colonel Martha Rainville, from the 158th Fighter Wing, became the first woman in guard history to be appointed as a state adjutant general.

CHAPTER 4
"These Things We Do So Others May Live"

Although the Army National Guard has no rescue and recovery teams, the Air National Guard has three units specifically used for such crucial missions. Each of these units remains faithful to their service code: "These Things We Do That Others May Live."

106th Rescue Squadron

The 106th Rescue Squadron, based at Suffolk County Airport in New York State, is the oldest Air National Guard unit in the country. Its origins can be traced to the 1st Aero Squadron, which formed in 1908. The 106th provides search and rescue assistance for an area that stretches from the northeastern United States, south to the Bahama Islands, and east to the Azores in the Atlantic. In addition, the 106th assists the New Hampshire Fish and Wildlife Service in conducting extensive mountain search and rescue operations. For mariners, hikers, skiers, and pilots in

The Perfect Storm

It was only recently that many people learned about the existence of the 160th Rescue Squadron. The publication of Sebastian Junger's book *The Perfect Storm* and the release of a film version told the story of a commercial fishing vessel and its crew who became lost during a great storm in October 1991. The storm was dubbed "perfect" because three weather systems collided to create a mammoth storm that caught weather forecasters unprepared. Based on actual events, the story also detailed the aborted rescue mission involving a five-man crew from the 106th. The crew had to "ditch" their helicopter in 70-foot (21.3 meter) waves and take their chances in the water until the Coast Guard reached them. Four of the five survived. The body of Technical Sergeant Rick Smith, a PJ, was never found.

distress, the 106th Rescue Wing is a lifeline. The unit is one of only a handful of rescue agencies able to penetrate the most remote areas of the world. As a result, it is frequently called upon to undertake the most difficult and hazardous missions.

In a newspaper article entitled "Elite rescuers are often last resort," written for the online magazine *Soundings*, Lieutenant

An Air National Guardsman examines the night-vision goggles on his helmet. Gear such as this special helmet is especially valuable to National Guard members in difficult operations.

Colonel James MacDougall explained that "the 106th is prepared to handle all types of crises." To date, the squad has saved nearly 300 lives. McDougall added that "combat rescue is really why the U.S. government formed the guard." But the skills needed for military missions can also be put to use in civilian rescues. John Spillane, a retired PJ also interviewed for the article, agreed. "When the authorities call, we're the last hope for many, and we take that very seriously."

The more memorable rescues that the 106th has undertaken include the longest over-water helicopter mission ever—fifteen hours nonstop—to save Ukrainian seamen after their freighter capsized and sank in the North Atlantic in December 1994. Despite heavy seas and hurricane-force winds, the fliers located a lone survivor bobbing in the water. PJ James "Doc" Dougherty jumped into the rough and raging sea and guided the seaman to a helicopter hoist.

The 106th has climbed mountains to rescue fallen hikers. They have flown exhaustive search and rescue missions, such as when TWA Flight 800 exploded in midair off Long Island in 1996 or when John F. Kennedy Jr.'s plane disappeared during a flight to Martha's Vineyard in July 1999. During a 1998 ice storm, the 106th checked on stranded New Yorkers, making sure they were safe and helped move them to shelter. Since the explosion of the space shuttle *Challenger* in 1986, the 106th has been on hand during every shuttle launch, prepared, if necessary, to rescue the astronauts. As a result of the terrorist attacks that took place on September 11, 2001, the 106th PJs are actively seeking new members, hoping that the recent attention to their efforts will help boost the number of recruits. Policemen and firefighters tend to make ideal PJs.

The 129th Rescue Squadron

The 129th Rescue Squadron, now based at Moffet Field, California, covers the West Coast of the United States. In 1999 alone, the 129th Rescue Squadron flew 2,300 hours during 1,268 missions and saved 280 lives. The members of the 129th perform rescues under a wide variety of conditions, from braving rough seas in the Pacific to the rugged terrain of the Sierra

Nevada. In 1990, the 129th, along with the 106th, also began to support the rescue coverage of NASA's space shuttle missions.

129th to the Rescue

One of the most common types of missions that the 129th has undertaken has been the medical evacuation of patients from merchant ships at sea. The 129th has completed more than forty of these high-risk lifesaving missions, which often consist of long-range, over-water flights. To ensure that helicopters do not run out of fuel, special supply planes hook up to the helicopters and refuel them while still in the air. Because the helicopters often do not have time or a place to land, skilled maneuvering by helicopter pilots and ships' captains is needed to transport the patients from the ships' decks. A milestone in this type of rescue was achieved on September 3, 1991, when members of the 129th recovered a sailor from a merchant vessel, marking the unit's 200th mission. Members of the 129th have also been involved in unusual rescues. In 1999, for example, a flight surgeon with the 129th unexpectedly performed emergency heart surgery on another physician at a research base in Antarctica.

One of the more exciting rescue missions involving the 129th occurred in October 1999. Working with the Coast Guard, the 129th rescued a civilian sailor en route from Hawaii to southern California, who was near death from congestive heart failure. After requesting assistance, the patient was transferred from his

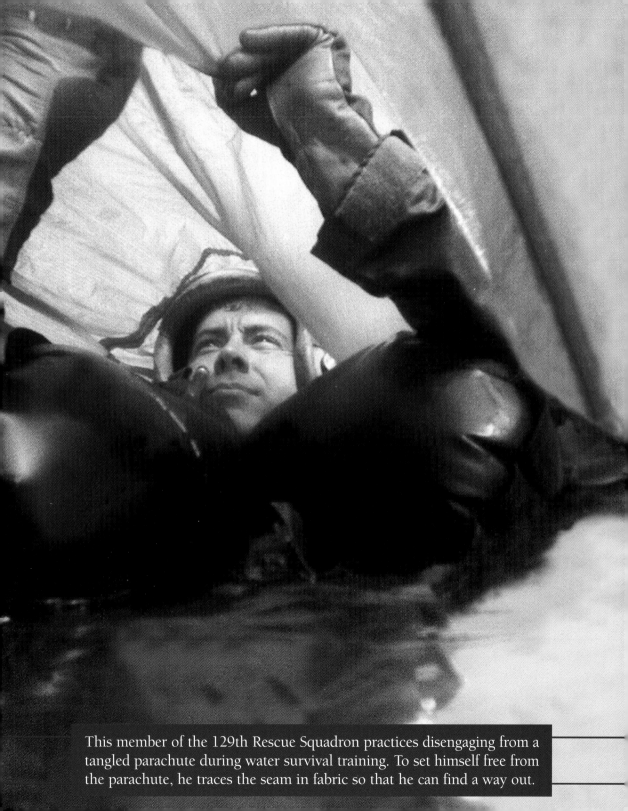

This member of the 129th Rescue Squadron practices disengaging from a tangled parachute during water survival training. To set himself free from the parachute, he traces the seam in fabric so that he can find a way out.

sailboat to a cargo vessel and then via a Coast Guard helicopter to a cutter. Aboard the cutter and still 600 miles offshore, the patient's condition worsened. The 129th responded by launching an HH-60 rescue helicopter and an HC-130 tanker. After in-flight refueling, the helicopter met the cutter and the patient was hoisted aboard, where 129th pararescuemen stabilized his condition. The patient was airlifted to Moffett Field and then transported by ambulance to Stanford Medical Center, where the admitting physician confirmed that the actions of the 129th had saved the sailor's life.

The Air National Guard often joins with the U.S. Coast Guard in rescue missions at sea.

The 210th Rescue Squadron

The third rescue and recovery squadron of the Air National Guard is the 210th Rescue Squadron, based in Anchorage, Alaska. Of the three rescue and recovery units, the 210th is by far the busiest. An all-volunteer unit, the 210th is the only rescue unit that allows civilians to join, and it is the only unit that is actively involved in civilian rescue on a daily basis. To date, the 210th has launched more than 724 missions resulting in 533 lives saved and 218 people assisted.

During times of war, the mission of the 210th changes. Then its responsibilities become combat search and rescue, locating and recovering downed fighter pilots. In times of peace, however, the unit routinely performs a twenty-four-hour Alaska theater search and rescue alert, which helps locate people missing (or in distress) throughout the state.

The more noteworthy accomplishments of the 210th include the rescue of the victims of a crashed Canadian forces C-130 near the North Pole in 1991 and combat search and rescue missions in Kuwait, Saudi Arabia, and Turkey for the coalition forces in Operations Northern and Southern Watch. The unit has also rescued mountain climbers trapped in the Denali Massif region of Alaska, located fishermen adrift in the perilous Bering Strait, found hunters lost in the Alaskan tundra, and rescued Navy SEALs who almost froze to death on a glacier the size of Rhode Island. The unit also found

Best of the Best

In September 1999, the 210th was the first Air National Guard unit to receive the prestigious Mackay Trophy, which is given annually for the most courageous and noteworthy flight in the U.S. Air Force. Previous winners include Hap Arnold, Eddie Rickenbacker, Jimmie Doolittle, and Chuck Yeager, a veritable "who's who" list in the history of American aviation. The unit also won the Jolly Green Rescue Mission of the Year Award.

General Michael Ryan (*far left*), chief of staff for the U.S. Air Force, presents the Mackey Trophy in 1999 to the Alaska Air National Guard 210th Rescue Squadron for rescuing six people from an airplane crash near Mount Spurr, Alaska.

time to act as the official U.S. representative to the annual Russia/U.S./Canada International Search and Rescue Exercises, with events held in each of those countries.

Always There, Always Ready, Always Vigilant

The events of September 11, 2001, made it clear that the Army and Air National Guard are important and valued resources. Without the skills and dedication of the thousands of men and women who make up the guard, the natural and man-made disasters that take place every year would take a much greater toll on property and lives. The quick response of the National Guard to crises large and small, personal and national, has helped Americans cope with devastating events.

The Air National Guard PJs are an important component of the National Guard team. Whether at work rescuing downed pilots during combat or stranded hikers in the mountains, the PJs, along with the rest of the rescue units, are often the last hope for desperate people. Whenever and wherever they are needed, the National Guard is always there, always ready, and always vigilant.

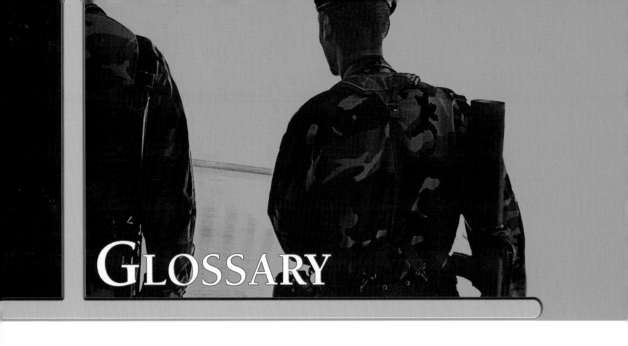

GLOSSARY

active Engaged in full-time service, especially in the armed forces.

armory A place where arms and military equipment are stored, or a place used for training reserve military personnel such as those in the National Guard.

brigade A large body of troops that often consists of one or more infantry or armored units and supporting troops.

Cold War A period of intense rivalry between the United States and the Soviet Union that never developed into a war. The Cold War lasted from the end of World War II in 1945 until 1990, when the Soviet Union collapsed.

company A group of soldiers, usually consisting of two or more platoons.

deployment The placement of soldiers at a particular location.

drill To train or exercise.

GED General equivalency diploma, which is similar to a high school diploma. Instead of course work, however, students take an examination to earn the GED.

Ground Zero The name given to the site on which the World Trade Center once stood; it refers to the center or origin of rapid, intense, or violent activity or change.

HC-130 tanker Also known as the HC-130 Hercules, this aircraft has almost limitless uses, including electronic surveillance, search and rescue, space-capsule recovery, helicopter refueling, and landing (with skis) on snow and ice.

HH-60 rescue helicopter A special helicopter known for its power and speed along with a long, seven-hour endurance. The helicopter is particularly suited for rescue work at low altitudes.

ING Inactive National Guard, or persons in an inactive status; they are attached to a specific National Guard unit but are not required to participate in training.

insurrection An act or instance of open revolt against civil authority or a government.

IRR Individual Ready Reserve; a term of service in the National Guard consisting mainly of individuals who have had previous military training and who may be called up for duty if necessary and must participate in monthly drills.

jurisdiction The power or right to exercise authority in certain territories or areas of government.

militia Part of the organized armed forces called to active duty only in an emergency, or a body of citizens organized for military service usually in a time of war or other crises.

morgue A place where the bodies of the dead are kept and examined.

regiment A military unit usually consisting of a number of battalions.

rescue hoist cable A rescue hook attached to a hoist cable that is used to assist rescue personnel in performing rescue operations from a helicopter. The cable can lift people and/or equipment during both sea and land helicopter rescues.

reserves Military forces that are available but that have not yet been called to active service or deployed for regular duty.

Saxon A member of a Germanic people who entered and conquered England in the fifth century AD and merged with them to form the Anglo-Saxon people.

FOR MORE INFORMATION

Web Sites

Due to the changing nature of Internet links, the Rosen
Publishing Group, Inc., has developed an online list of Web
sites related to the subject of this book. This site is updated
regularly. Please use this link to access the list:

http://www.rosenlinks.com/csro/aang/

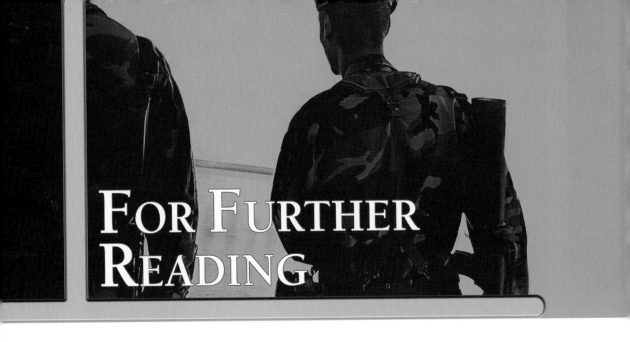

FOR FURTHER READING

Doubler, Michael D., Jown W. Lisman Jr., and Donald M. Goldstein. *National Guard: An Illustrated History of America's Citizen Soldier*. London: Brassey's Inc., 2002.

Duncan, Stephen M. *Citizen Warriors: America's National Guard and Reserve Forces & the Politics of National Security*. Navato, CA: Presidio Press, 1997.

Francillon, Rene S., and Stan Moins. *The United States Air National Guard*. Westport, CT: Airtime Publishing, 1993.

Hall, George. *Air Guard: America's Flying Militia*. Novato, CA: Presidio Press, 1990.

BIBLIOGRAPHY

Brehm, Jack, and Pete Nelson. *That Others May Live: The True Story of a PJ, a Member of America's Most Daring Rescue Force.* New York: Crown Publishers, 2000.

Drumsta, Raymond. "NY Guard Soldiers at Ground Zero." National Guard Press Release, October 10, 2001. Retrieved April 20, 2002 (http://www.ngb.dtic.mil/news/2001/10/10/groundzero.shtml).

Drury, Bob. *The Rescue Season: The Heroic Story of Parajumpers on the Edge of the World.* New York: Simon & Schuster, 2001.

Gilmore, Gerry J. "Bush Authorizes Guard and Reserve Call-Ups." American Forces Information Services, September 14, 2001. Retrieved May 1, 2002 (http://www.defenselink.mil/news/Sep2001/n09142001_200109148.html).

Goddard, JoAnn W. "Elite Rescuers Are Often Last Resort." *Soundings.* Retrieved May 1, 2002 (http://www.soundingsonline.com/archive.story/1407.html).

Gross, Charles Joseph. *Prelude to Total Force: The Air National Guard 1943–1969*. Washington D.C.: Office of Air Force History, 1985.

Haskell, Bob. "Determined Guard." National Guard Press Release, September 24, 2001. Retrieved April 20, 2002 (http://www.ngb.dtic.mil/news/2001/09/24/det_guard.shtml).

Haskell, Bob. "Empire Guards." National Guard Press Release, September 24, 2001. Retrieved April 18, 2002 (http://www.ngb.dtic.mil/news/2001/09/24/emp_guard.shtml).

Haskell, Bob. "Guard Soldiers Help East Coast Dig Out from Blizzard." *Army Link News*. January 27 2000. Retrieved April 18, 2002 (http://www.dtic.mil/armylink/news/Jan2000/a20000127ngsnow.html).

Haskell, Bob. "Medical Heroes." National Guard Press Release, September 18, 2001. Retrieved April 16, 2002 (http://www.ngb.dtic.mil/news/2001/09/18/med_heroes.shtml).

Mahon, John K. *History of the Militia and National Guard*. New York: Macmillan Publishing, 1983.

"Message from General Weaver." National Guard Press Release, September 17, 2001. Retrieved April 12, 2002 (http://www.ngb.dtic.mil/news/2001/09/17/weaver.shtml).

Morando, Paul. "Crisis Redefines These New York Guardsmen." American Forces Information Service, September 24, 2001.

Retrieved April 12, 2002 (http://www.defenselink.mil/news/
Sep2001/n09242001_200109248.html).

Office of the Assistant Secretary of Defense. "Population
Representation in the Military Services," November 2000.
Retrieved April 14, 2002 (http://dticaw.dtic.mil/prhome/
poprep99/html/chapter5/c5-re-occupations.htm).

Powers, Jon, and Robert Stephenson. "On Guard in America:
The National Guard Provides Homeland Defense." *USA
Today* magazine, March 2002, Vol. 130, Issue 2682, p. 10.

Rhem, Kathleen T., Sgt. "Guard Civil Support Team Put to
the Test in New York City." American Forces Information
Services, September 14, 2001. Retrieved April 14, 2002
(http://www.defenselink.mil/news/Sep2001/n09142001_
200109143.html).

Schmidt, Karl. "Mission One." National Guard
Press Release, September 14, 2001. Retrieved April 12,
2002 (http://www.ngb.dtic.mil/news/2001/09/14/
missionone.shtml).

Simon, Seena, and Mark C. Brinkley. "First to Act." *Army Times*,
September 24, 2001, Vol. 62, No.9, pp. 22–23.

"09/12/2001—National Guard Responds to Terrorism."
National Guard Press Release. Retrieved April 20, 2002
(http://www.ngb.dtic.mil/news/2001/09/12/terrorism.shtml).

INDEX

A

active duty training (ADT), 35
Aerospace Rescue and Recovery Group
    (ARRG), 30
Air National Guard, about the, 24–30
Alaska theater search and rescue
    alert, 51
American Revolution, 15, 16, 17
Anchorage, Alaska, 51
Armed Services Aptitude Battery
    (ASVAB), 33, 35

B

Bahama Islands, 43
Bosnia, 21
Boston, Massachusetts, 6, 14
Bush, President George W., 8

C

Challenger, 46
Civil Support Team (CST), 7
Civil War, 17–18, 27
Coast Guard, 48, 50
Cold War, 27
Congress, 18, 24
Continental army, 16

D

Dick Act, 18

F

Federal Bureau of Investigation (FBI), 7
1st Aero Company, 26, 43
Franklin, Benjamin, 15
French and Indian War, 15

G

GI Bill, 34

H

HC-130 aircraft, 25, 50
HH-60 helicopters, 25, 50
History of the Militia and National Guard, 15

I

Inactive National Guard (ING), 33
Individual Ready Reserve (IRR), 33

K

Korean War, 21, 27
Kuwait, 51

L

Liberty Island State Park, 8

M

Mahon, John K., 15
Militia Act of 1792, 16
Moffet Field, California, 47, 50

N

National Defense Act of 1916, 19
National Defense Act of 1920, 20
National Guard,
    history of, 14–23, 26–28, 30
    qualifications for, 31–33
    standards of, 18, 20
    training for, 35–38, 39
    women in, 36, 40–42, 47
Noriega, Manuel, 28

O

106th Rescue Squadron, 43–47, 48
129th Rescue Squadron, 47–50
Operation Desert Storm, 21, 28, 40
Operation Just Cause, 27–28
Operation Noble Eagle, 8
Operations Northern and Southern
    Watch, 51
Operation Urgent Fury, 27

P

pararescue jumpers (PJs), 29, 30, 39,
    46–47, 53
Pentagon, 4, 11, 13

R

Roosevelt, President Franklin D., 26
Roosevelt, President Theodore, 19
Rough Riders, 19
Russia/U.S./Canada International Search
    and Rescue Exercises, 53

S

Saudi Arabia, 40, 51
search and rescue missions,
    history of, 29
Spanish American War, 18, 19

T

Turkey, 51
204th Combat Engineering
    Battalion, 9
210th Rescue Squadron, 51–53

V

Vietnam War, 21, 27, 29

W

War Department, 20
War of 1812, 16
War of Independence, 15–16, 17
World Trade Center, 4, 6–7, 9,
    11, 13
World War I, 21
World War II, 21, 26, 29

About the Author

Meg Greene is a writer and historian. She received a B.S. in history from Lindenwood College, an M.A. in history from the University of Nebraska at Omaha, and an M.S. in historic preservation from the University of Vermont. She is the author of fourteen books and serves as contributing editor of "History for Children" at Suite101.com. Ms. Greene makes her home in Virginia.

Photo Credits

Cover © Timothy Clary/Corbis; pp. 1, 8, 12 © Corbis; p. 5 © TimePix; p. 20 © Hulton/Archive/Getty Images; pp. 22, 38, 41, 52 © AP/Wide World Photos; p. 25 © Toby Talbot/AP/Wide World Photos; p. 28 © Ed Andrieski/AP/Wide World Photos; p. 32 © Richard Benke/AP/Wide World Photos; p. 37 © Ron Winn/AP/Wide World Photos; p. 45 © Ed Bailey/AP/Wide World Photos; pp. 49, 50 © United States Air Force.

Editor

Annie Sommers

Designer

Nelson Sá